The Lost and Found Game

by Judy Nayer
Illustrated by Leanne Franson

16 17 18 19 20   10 09

1-800-321-3106
www.pearsonlearning.com

CONTENTS

Baseball Time Again

Jody Martin and Ben Stubbs hurried to join the rest of the team on the Quincy Park baseball field. It was a perfect day. It was the best kind of day for their first practice of the Little League season. Jody tucked her long hair under her cap. Ben punched his hand into his mitt.

Ben walked over to his friend Brad Ming. Brad was sitting on the field, reading.

"Brad!" teased Ben. "I know you're a great ball player, but I don't think you can read and play baseball at the same time!"

Brad looked up and smiled. "I was just waiting for you to get here."

Jody saw Tina Perez hop out of a car as her mom dropped her off. "Over here, Tina!" she called to her friend.

All the players started talking at once. They wanted to know who would be playing what position.

Everyone quieted down when Coach Reed started to talk. "OK, Quincy Cougars! Are you ready to play ball?"

"Yeah!" everyone shouted together.

The team started to line up, but Coach Reed stopped them. "One more thing," he added. "I might as well get the bad news out of the way. The company that usually pays for our uniforms has moved away from Quincy. We're looking for a new sponsor, but for now we don't have money for new uniforms."

Everyone groaned.

"But how can we wear the old uniforms?" asked Jody. "My uniform has holes in it!"

"My uniform is going to be way too small," said Ben. "I grew since last season."

Coach Reed shook his head. "Maybe some of you can think of a way we can raise money," he said. "In the meantime, you don't need your uniforms to practice, do you?"

In a few minutes, they were having a good time playing ball. However, in the back of everyone's mind was the question, "What are we going to do about uniforms?"

A Good Idea

When baseball practice was over, Jody's mom was there waiting for her. Jody said goodbye to her friends.

"How was practice?" Mrs. Martin asked.

"Great!" said Jody. "How was the police station?"

"Just fine," Mrs. Martin said. She worked for the Quincy Police Department.

Then Jody remembered what had happened. "I take back what I said about practice. It wasn't great. Coach Reed says we can't get new uniforms until we get a new sponsor," she added.

Mrs. Martin thought a bit. "Hmmm," she said. "We'll think of something. I'll ask at the station house. Maybe someone will have an idea."

"We're going to look a little silly in those old uniforms. They're all worn out, and some of them will be too small," said Jody.

When they reached their block, Jody saw
a banner. She read:

Third Street Fair
Saturday, June 12

"Hey, Mom! There's going to be a street
fair right here on our street!" said Jody,
pointing to the banner.

"I heard about it this morning," said Mrs. Martin. "It should be fun. Say. . . that gives me an idea. You and your friends can set up a table at the fair to raise money."

"OK, Mom. But how could we raise money with a table?" Jody teased.

Mrs. Martin laughed. "You could sell something. People sell all kinds of things at a street fair," she said.

"But what can we sell?" asked Jody.

Mrs. Martin was quiet until they got inside the house. "I have another idea," she said as she stopped in the kitchen. "You can collect rummage from all the neighbors. Then you can sell the rummage at the fair."

"Sounds great, Mom," said Jody. "I have one more question. What's rummage?"

Mrs. Martin laughed again. "That is a funny word, isn't it?" she said. "Rummage is used things people don't want anymore."

Jody was still a little confused. "You mean," she asked, "people will buy other people's old stuff?"

"Sure!" said Mrs. Martin. "You'd be surprised what people will buy."

"Maybe we'll be able to get new uniforms after all!" said Jody.

Getting to Work

The next day, Jody got to school just as the bell rang. She had to take her seat before she could talk to Ben, Brad, or Tina.

In class, they were studying ancient history. Their teacher, Ms. Ramos, was asking questions.

"Can anyone tell me where Egypt is?" asked Ms. Ramos.

Brad's hand shot up in the air. He always knew the answers.

"Yes, Brad?" asked Ms. Ramos.

"Egypt is a country in northern Africa," Brad said.

"That's right," said Ms. Ramos, as she pointed to Africa on a large map of the world. "For our last ancient history unit this school year, we will be studying Africa. And, we'll have a chance to learn more about Egypt and the rest of Africa when we go on our field trip to the Quincy Museum of Natural History."

"Yeah! Field trip!" everyone cheered.

At lunch, Jody rejoined her friends in the cafeteria. As they ate, she told them all about her mother's idea. Everyone thought it was a great plan. They began to think of all the old stuff they had at home that they might donate to the sale. When it was time to go back to class, they agreed to get together after school to work on their plan.

That afternoon, Jody, Ben, Tina, and Brad went to Jody's house to work on the rummage sale. First, they decided what they wanted to say. Then they rewrote the words on a sign.

RUMMAGE SALE

Help us raise money for new baseball uniforms.
We are collecting items for the street fair.
Bring us your used books, clothing, toys, and any other things you want to donate.
We will pick up, too!

To finish the sign, they wrote their names at the bottom and the name of their baseball team. They wanted to make sure that everyone in the neighborhood knew who was doing the collecting and why.

Then the kids all went to Eddie's Bodega down the block. Eddie's was the little grocery store on the corner.

"Hi, Eddie!" said Jody.

"Hola!" Eddie answered with a big smile.

"Guess what?" said Ben. "We're collecting rummage to sell at the street fair."

"We're trying to make money so we can buy new baseball uniforms for the Quincy Cougars," added Tina and Brad.

"Do you have any boxes we could have to put the things in?" asked Jody.

"You came to the right place!" said Eddie. "I have a lot of empty cardboard boxes. So you can help yourselves."

Eddie pointed toward the storage room at the back of the store. The kids took as many boxes as they could carry.

"Come back tomorrow," Eddie said. "I'll have the best rummage you've ever seen ready and waiting."

"Thanks, Eddie!" they called as they left the store. "Don't forget to come to the fair!"

The Mystery Box

The next day was Saturday. Jody, Ben, Tina, and Brad met at Jody's house. Together they went back to Eddie's Bodega. He gave them four big boxes full of great stuff. He also gave them a roll of blank, peel-off stickers they could use as price tags.

The kids brought the boxes back to Jody's house. Then, they sat on the front steps with their sign.

A lot of people stopped as they were walking by. At first, no one brought them anything. They just read the sign, and walked on. By the afternoon, though, neighbors were bringing them things for the rummage sale.

It wasn't long before the boxes were filling up. "Wow!" said Jody as she took a lamp from Tina's mother. "I don't know if all this stuff will even fit on our table!"

On Sunday afternoon, Jody's grandfather came. He asked the kids what they were up to. They pointed to their boxes full of old stuff and told him about their plan.

"You're collecting rummage?" asked Jody's grandfather. "Why, I've got a whole attic full of old stuff. You're all welcome to come to my house and take anything you want. In fact, you'd be doing me a favor to clear the place out. It's a bit disordered up there."

Jody and her friends were excited. Jody ran inside to talk to her mom. "Can we go to Grandpa's?" she asked.

"Sure," said Mrs. Martin. "I'll take you over there. That way we can put the things in our car."

In a short while they were at Jody's grandfather's house. Jody led them up the narrow stairs to the attic.

"Look at this place!" said Brad. "It's full of great stuff!"

The kids started to fill boxes with all kinds of old things. They uncovered books, watches, dishes, kitchen gadgets, some golf clubs, a fishing pole, and an old radio. Just as they were about to pick up the boxes to leave, Jody noticed a small box in the corner.

"I think I can carry this one, too," she said, adding the box to the top of her pile.

Back at Jody's house, the kids got busy sorting the boxes. They made a price tag for each item.

They made sure the prices weren't too high. If they were too expensive, no one would want to buy anything.

Then Tina dug into a box and held up something long and narrow. It was wooden, and it looked like a case of some kind.

"What is this?" she asked.

Tina opened it up. Inside were little colored stones in different compartments.

"I don't know," said Ben. "It looks very old."

"It sure does," said Brad. "Maybe it's used to count things, like the Chinese abacus."

"Let's set our mystery box aside," said Jody. "We can't put a price on it if we don't know what it is."

The kids continued working until they had priced nearly everything. They were very tired when they finished.

"I think I'm going home to get some rest," Brad said. "I don't want to be too tired for the school field trip tomorrow."

CHAPTER 5

The Field Trip

First thing Monday morning, Ms. Ramos's class was ready for the field trip! When they got off the bus in front of the Quincy Museum of Natural History, everyone gathered on the sidewalk. Then they went into the museum where they were met by the museum guide.

"We're going to the African exhibit first," said Ms. Ramos.

Tina looked around excitedly when she saw the African exhibit. "Wow," she said. "Look at all these ancient artifacts!"

"What are artifacts?" Ben asked.

"That's a good question," said the museum guide. "Artifacts are objects left behind by people who made them long ago. They may be hundreds, even thousands, of years old."

All of a sudden, something caught Ben's eye. He grabbed Jody's arm.

"Look, Jody!" whispered Ben. "That wooden case looks like our mystery box!"

Jody carefully studied the old wooden case with stones that Ben was pointing to. "It sure looks like it!" she finally said.

Ben started to read the information card next to it. It said:

These ancient games have been played in Africa for more than 3,000 years.

"Wow! It's a game!" Ben exclaimed. Brad and Tina hurried over. They all began to read the card.

Then Ms. Ramos came over and the rest of the class moved over to where Ben and Jody were standing.

"Look at the game inside the case," said Jody. "When we were collecting things for our rummage sale, we found something that looks just like this wooden case."

The museum guide explained, "That game is called Wari. The earliest boards were found in Egypt. Today, the game is played all over Africa, and in many other parts of the world, too."

He continued. "If you have a board that looks like this one, it certainly isn't rummage. It could be very valuable."

"Maybe it's worth a lot of money," Ben said. "Maybe it's worth enough to get uniforms for our whole team."

"Let's wait until we know more about it," Brad said. "It's not a good idea to count your chickens before they hatch."

"What does that mean?" Ben asked.

"It means, let's not buy the uniforms before we have the money," Brad replied.

The rest of the trip continued without any interruptions. All of the kids enjoyed learning more about how people lived long ago. Time passed quickly, and soon it was time to reboard the bus.

After they got back to school and the final bell of the day rang, Jody, Ben, Tina, and Brad met on the sidewalk outside.

"Let's go to my house," Jody said. "I want to take a closer look at that game."

When they got to Jody's, the kids found the game.

"That's one of the boxes from my grandfather's attic," Jody said. "Maybe Grandpa can tell us about it."

Jody explained the whole story to her mother, who called Jody's grandfather.

"Dad," she said, "the kids say they found an old Wari board in your attic when they came to pick up some rummage. They say it could be valuable."

"They're right," said Jody's grandfather. "I misplaced it a long time ago and have been wondering where it was. I'll be right over," he said.

It wasn't long before Jody's grandfather arrived. He sat with the kids at the dining room table and explained that the board was indeed very old. It wasn't as ancient as the one in the museum, but it was very valuable to him.

"It's a good thing we didn't sell it at the rummage sale," said Tina.

"It sure is," said Jody's grandfather.

"I want to know how to play," said Ben.

"I'll teach all of you," said Grandpa.

Grandpa talked, moving the stones from cup to cup. They were all having fun learning how to play the great new game. Little did they know just how great the game would turn out to be!

Another Good Idea

The next day, with her grandfather's permission, Jody brought the Wari board to school. Jody pointed out how her game was a lot like the one they had seen in the museum. Then she told them how her grandfather had taught her, Ben, Brad, and Tina how to play. After she finished talking, a lot of kids asked questions.

After school, Jody and Ben started walking home together. Then Jody stopped at the corner.

"I have to go this way," she said. "I have to return the Wari board to Grandpa."

"Too bad," said Ben. "We won't be able to play anymore."

"Maybe Grandpa will let us come over some time and play it with him. See you tomorrow," Jody said as she walked down the street.

Ben was busy, too. He had to help his father, who owned the Quincy Bakery.

When Ben got to the bakery he called out, "Hi, Dad!" He put down his backpack and went behind the counter for one of his favorite cookies.

"Wow!" he said, looking at a huge stack of egg cartons.

"We have to get all these eggs into the big refrigerator," said Mr. Stubbs. "Oh, and recheck the cartons for me. We don't want any broken eggs left in them."

"Sure, Dad," said Ben. He finished his cookie and got to work. Carefully he took a carton and opened it. He fingered the eggs to make sure none were broken. "Two, four, six, eight, ten, twelve," he said.

Ben opened and closed carton after carton. Suddenly, it hit him. "This is just like a Wari board! It has six spaces on each side!"

Ben continued counting. Then he stopped again. "I bet we can make Wari boards out of empty egg cartons!"

"What's that?" called Mr. Stubbs. "Are you talking to yourself?" he laughed.

"Nothing, Dad," said Ben. He didn't want to take time to explain. "Will you please save these egg cartons for me? I need them for a project."

After Ben finished his work, he went to look for the cartons his dad had told him about. He took a few with him. He couldn't wait to talk to his friends.

Teamwork

The next morning at school, Ben met Tina, Brad, and Jody in the schoolyard. They could tell he was excited.

"I have a great idea," Ben said. He quickly told them about the egg cartons. "I thought we could make a lot of Wari games and sell them at the fair," he said.

"We'll work like a team," he went on. "I'll get the empty cartons. Jody will paint them. Tina can get stones. Brad will . . ."

Jody interrupted. "Wait a minute," she said. "If we're going to work like a team, then we should all decide what we're going to do, right?"

Ben slowed down. Everyone liked the idea, including Jody. She just liked to think things through.

"I know," said Tina. "We can use beans instead of stones. My mom has a big jar of dried pinto beans."

Brad did the math in his head. "You'll need 48 beans for each board," he said. "And I know what I can do. I can rewrite the directions for how to play on my computer and print them out. Then we can include directions inside each game."

"Good thinking!" said Jody. "Ben, can you bring the cartons to my house?"

"Sure!" said Ben. "This will be great!"

After school, Jody worked on turning an empty egg carton into a Wari board. It wasn't as easy as it looked. She glued colored paper on the bottom of the cups so they wouldn't be so deep. Then she painted the whole carton with shiny brown paint that wouldn't chip. She even painted African designs all over it. By the end of the afternoon she had finished it.

Jody brought her homemade Wari board to school. Without letting anyone else see, she showed it to her friends.

"That looks great!" said Ben.

"I really like the designs," Tina said. "They make the board look special. I brought some beans. Maybe we can try playing the game to see how it works."

"Let's wait until later," Brad said. "We don't want anyone to see our game before the fair."

"We have a problem," Jody said. "It took me all afternoon to make just this one game. How are we going to make them all in time for the fair on Saturday? Today's Thursday, and we have baseball practice after school. That leaves only one day!"

"Don't worry," said Ben. "We'll all help. Remember . . . teamwork!"

At baseball practice, Jody, Ben, Tina, and Brad told Coach Reed and the team all about the rummage sale.

"You wouldn't believe how much stuff we've collected," said Jody.

"We're going to make enough money to buy all our new uniforms!" said Ben.

Coach Reed said, "That's wonderful. But don't be too disappointed if you don't make enough money. Uniforms for the whole team won't be inexpensive."

Ben grinned at his friends. Coach Reed didn't know about the Wari boards yet.

Friday evening everyone gathered at
Jody's house. Even Ben's dad and Tina's
mom came.

"I wanted to know where all my egg
cartons were going to," laughed Mr. Stubbs.

"And I wanted to know where Tina was
taking all those beans," said Mrs. Perez.

"I made a bunch of copies of the game
directions," Brad said. He held up a stack
of printed sheets of paper.

Jody's mom put all the supplies on the dining room table. Everyone had a different job to do. By the end of the evening, they had made 40 Wari boards! The newly painted cartons were lined up on the table and on the kitchen counter as the paint dried. Tina and Brad were just about finished counting the beans for each game. They put the beans in small plastic bags.

"I bet we sell out in no time," Ben smiled.

CHAPTER 8

The Street Fair

Early Saturday morning, Ben, Tina, Brad, and their parents met at Jody's house again. Everyone helped reload the boxes and, of course, the Wari boards. Then they carried the boxes downstairs to the street for the rummage sale.

At the fair, they set up two tables. One table was for rummage. On the other table, they set up the Wari games. Brad had made a banner to hang behind the tables. It said:

HELP THE QUINCY COUGARS
BUY NEW UNIFORMS!

He also made two smaller signs for the tables. One said RUMMAGE SALE, and the other said WARI GAMES $4.00.

Things got pretty busy once the fair began. Ben had borrowed his dad's cash box to keep the money in. Tina was in charge of adding up the purchases and giving change. Jody was in charge of the Wari table, and Brad and Ben made sure the rummage table was kept full.

Lots of kids came by. They had seen Jody's grandfather's Wari board in class, and they all wanted one of their own. It wasn't long before all the games were sold.

Tina added it up. "We've made $160.00 on Wari boards alone!"

For the rest of the day they took orders for more Wari boards. By the time they had made and delivered those, they would have even more money for the uniforms.

The rummage sale was a big success, too. People bought things the kids never thought anyone would buy.

"Don't worry!" Jody's grandfather said. "I'm only buying things I need."

Two weeks later, the Quincy Cougars were sitting on the bench. They were ready for their first game of the season.

"These new uniforms are awesome!" said Ben, looking around at his team.

"Thanks to Jody, Tina, Ben and Brad," said Coach Reed.

"Let's hear a cheer. Without them, we never would have been able to get these uniforms," Coach Reed said.

Everyone cheered. Just then, a clap of thunder was heard overhead. The cheers turned to groans.

"Oh, no!" said Brad, looking up at the sky. "If it rains, we won't be able to play."

"That's OK," said Ben cheerfully. Everyone looked at him in surprise. If Ben couldn't play baseball, he was usually unhappy about it.

"If it rains, we can do something else," Ben said.

"Like what?" the other kids asked him.

"Like Wari," Ben said. He pulled out his egg carton Wari board from his backpack. Then he held up a little bag of beans.

"Now we have another game to play on rainy days," he said.

GLOSSARY

ancient (AYN shent) of great age; very old

attic (AT ihk) a space in a house that is just below the roof and above the other rooms

confused (kun FYOOZD) mixed up

donate (DOH nayt) to make a gift of

exhibit (eg ZIHB iht) things shown publicly

gadgets (GAJ ihtz) small tools made to do a certain job

museum (myoo ZEE uhm) a building or room where a collection of objects is kept and displayed

permission (pur MIHSH un) the act of letting someone do something

sponsor (SPAHN sur) a person or group who helps another person or group by paying expenses

valuable (VAL yoo uh bul) having great worth